Also by David Lehman

Yeshiva Boys

Poems

David Lehman

SCRIBNER

New York   London   Toronto   Sydney

SCRIBNER
A Division of Simon & Schuster, Inc.
1230 Avenue of the Americas
New York, NY 10020

First Scribner hardcover edition November 2009

SCRIBNER and design are registered trademarks of The Gale Group, Inc., used under license by Simon & Schuster, Inc., the publisher of this work.

For information about special discounts for bulk purchases, please contact Simon & Schuster Special Sales at 1-866-506-1949 or business@simonandschuster.com.

The Simon & Schuster Speakers Bureau can bring authors to your live event. For more information or to book an event, contact the Simon & Schuster Speakers Bureau at 1-866-248-3049 or visit our website at www.simonspeakers.com.

DESIGNED BY ERICH HOBBING

Text set in Sabon

Manufactured in the United States of America

10 9 8 7 6 5 4 3 2 1

Library of Congress Control Number: 2009024143

ISBN 978-1-4391-5444-1

In memoriam
Joseph Lehman,
1912–1971

Anne Lehman,
1915–2009

CONTENTS

I

Yeshiva Boys

Part I

On Purpose

"What is the purpose of your poems?"
I'm glad you asked me that
as I stand here in Mr. Ferry's eleventh-grade English class
in Lake Forest High School
I have given a lot of thought to "purpose"
Walking with a purposeful air in New York City
has obvious benefits in the chill of the night with wind
and it's even better when it's no bluff
you do know where you're going
from day to day
and you know when it's over
so it's like a story with a beginning middle and end
yet you could not tell me the purpose
of high school humiliation and I could not tell you
the purpose of this dream where you get up from these desks
and go to college and become lawyers or failures or soccer moms
and when you wake up you will have no recollection
of this encounter in the dark but it will linger nevertheless
and bring refreshment to your soul

A Dedication

To Henri Michaux, whose "major ordeals
of the mind and countless minor ones"
have hurt me like a wound that heals
leaving no scar, I dedicate my four major rhododendrons

and minor myrtle, day lilies, dill, rosemary,
and the underrated daisies that your mind
stores up for an afternoon nap in February,
an underrated time of year in New York, a minor time

of day, and you wonder what it means to be
an underrated pinch hitter or out-of-work mime
or even "a minor Atlantic Goethe," who told me

 a minority opinion the majority of the time
is an underrated pleasure but an overrated wish
(as is the mind's ability to vanish)

Confessions of a Mask

These are the confessions of a mask.
I looked in the mirror and saw a ghost.
Of all lost causes I miss this one the most.
These are the questions you must not ask.

These are the oaks that once stood here.
And shall the earth be all of paradise
That we will know? Roll the dice;
These are the nights when praise turns into fear.

These are the memories of a man without a past.
Oh, I kept the first for another day!
Therefore, let us sport us while we may.
These are the reveries of a man who climbed the mast.

These are the reasons the student failed the course.
Some mute inglorious Milton
Against windmills did go tilting.
These are the seasons of a girl and her horse.

These are the days of sunlight and high skies.
Did she put on his knowledge with his power?
Unseal the earth and lift love in her shower.
These are the ways the humble man is wise.

These are the questions you must not ask.
Was it a vision or a waking dream?
Let be be finale of seem.
These are the confessions of a mask.

The Shield of a Greeting

for J.A.

Ashes that survive the aftermath of fire
Bury the past bravely, retaining
Only those messages that are least decipherable
And therefore most desirable
To be sung by the bright-eyed few remaining
Voices of our frankly foolish choir.

—*December 3, 1975*

Salutation

"I'll have to ask you to repeat that.
What did you say?" "No problem.
I said you're quite a young man to have
developed a case of amnesia as advanced
as yours." But he was thinking of writers
who bare their souls in popular magazines.

They confess their vices in such magazines
as "Spank," "Ms. Fortune," and "Beat That."
That's the thing about ambitious middle-aged writers
who used to be young: each has a secret problem,
and if they confess it, they think it will advance
their careers. All believe they have

not been appreciated enough by lovers who have
cheated on them as by philistine editors of magazines
who commission out of hope and edit out of fear. The advance
on their next book is spent at lunch, and that
isn't funny. Six out of ten have a drinking problem.
But when was that a bar to their need to be writers?

To write a best-seller is every writer's
fantasy, and if you write three or four you'll have
retirement options beyond the usual. But look at the problems
standing between you and your modest goal of magazine
publication, a tenure-track appointment, and that
sexy partner you're trying to impress. Advance

praise has to be got from writers who've advanced
to the fore. To join the ranks of such writers
may, however, seem a less worthy goal now that
you've met the vain jerks who have
seized the means of production. Still, these problems
exist in order for you to solve them, and in your own magazine—

the apotheosis of a modern avant-garde magazine—
you may disdain to publish anyone save those with the most advanced
views, though that path may create yet more problems.
For often the most talented writers are not the writers
you'd like to have dinner with, have drinks with, even have
an elevator conversation with, about this, the other, or that.

To sum up: to publish a piece in that imaginary magazine,
you have to have an advanced case of something,
some marvelous incurable problem that will make you a writer.

Election Day

E. B. White said democracy
is a letter to the editor and
I'm not sure I agree though I
love letters to the editor
particularly loony ones that
begin by quoting Bob Dylan's
"Like a Rolling Stone" and end
by endorsing "nobody" for
president ("If nobody wins
nobody loses") but when I
think of democracy in America
I think not of Tocqueville but
of *The Great McGinty*
a great Preston Sturges movie
where the big city hero now
a bartender recounts how
he, a bum, got paid to vote early,
vote often, and so impressed
the machine boss that he rose
to become an alderman
then the mayor of the city
then governor and would have
kept the job, too, if he hadn't
(thanks to do-gooder wife)
tried to do some good for
the people some think

the moral is that politics
is crooked but I think it's
that anyone can grow up
to become governor

The Road to Help

A thong of beauty is a joy forever.
The panty's over; it's time to call it a lay.
The shadow of the come of pleasure
and naked singles of the world
are here, under the bush, with her hair.
For Hamlet and Lear are queer.

Myself am help. Shall I part my bare behind?
God bless the grind! I shall walk softly there.
The paths of Laurie lead but to the grove
of coral babes and amber studs
with black belts in the marital arts.
Of his boners are coral made.

"Dope" is the thing with feathers.
The love of monkey is the root of all evil.
Was she a virgin or a waking dream?
"Deaf" was all he answered.
Tis better to seek, to find, and now to yield
than never to have lust at all.

Coded Love Poem

O I love Sadie whether laved or furry
As you move rock whether ball or bit.
I won't be a pig, you won't be sorry;
you won't be a prig, and I won't worry.

O I love mitts whether curved or not.
I run outdoors, mad to be in contact with it.
With what? Even in winter you'd be hot.
We have one gun only. Who will be shot?

O I love ships and jelly, ties and brass,
As heat though white is red in thought.
Hide with me beneath the house, my lass.
We'll pass notes in the last row of the class.

If it's night we will buck until freak of day,
If it's day we will rock until fast of night,
And all night long and all through the day,
We'll make love run (make out, make hay).

Summer Romance

"You're giving me a complex,"
Electra joked. Plato was barking up the wrong——
and sang in the wrong——
but came the point of crisis in the song
and they felt free
and so did we
in the ensuing outbreak of oral——
which we considered moral.

He knew her secret.
Why did she always find
it in the last place she looked?
It was a necessary prop, like a cigarette.
It was the nature of the beast
with two backs. What happened next
was a second round of oral——
which some considered abnormal.

Life with Electra was a brilliant quarrel
or a chase scene ending in the wrecks
of both cars, hers and his, after they sinned.
She got to choose between her ex
and his why. But that was the least
of her concerns in the wind
(one puff and you're hooked)
where reality was a province of the mind.

Hopper

The disappearance of a cat is a good omen,
He said when she told him that hers was missing
A week after moving into her new house.
Cats in captivity violate the natural order,
He said. They should be out prowling, left
To fend for themselves in the streets and alleys
Of cities whose night life depends on them,
On having them in the picture along with a cigarette,
A lamppost, the lid of an aluminum garbage can,
A police siren, an off-duty nightclub dancer
In a flimsy frock, with a run
In her nylons. A searchlight, a spotlight.
Strapless. The theater poster on the wall.

Hymn to Man

Love will last, or it won't, in this or some other town.
—*The Threepenny Opera*

Therefore, let's praise man, the animal that plans his next infidelity before completing the one at hand, in this or some other city.

Man is the mammal that blames his mother and curses his father.

And in that case, what is woman?

Woman is man with a few things added and a few things taken away.

Man is (choose one) more or less afraid of death than any other mammal.

Man (a) talks more (b) listens less than any other manimal.

Man exists (a) to fulfill the divine command (b) to affirm his own existence (c) for no good reason (d) for no reason, good or bad.

And in that case, what is woman?

Woman is the mother of man and the daughter of woman and the sister that rescued the boy in the rushes and the unsatisfied wife in a remote province, Manitoba or Alberta, the deceived wife too busy to notice or the undeceived wife who pretends not to notice or the wife who stiffens her husband's resolve or none of these or all, muse or concubine, nun or hausfrau.

Man thinks man as a category embraces woman. Woman believes woman contains man.

Man is the mammal that goes to museums to look not at the paintings but at the woman looking at them.

Woman is the heroine. Or woman is heroin. Woman is two sides of the eternal triangle. Or woman is the radius of the circle squared. Man is the diameter of the circle times two.

Man is the Arthur Dimmesdale Professor of Serial Adultery who writes a boring book on *The Scarlet Letter* and dedicates it to his wife.

Woman is the expensive call girl who gets to recover her virginity and make a career out of it.

Man is the only animal who thinks he is the only animal.

Woman is the only animal who thinks.

Woman is the part of man that beholds the paragon of the animals and calls it a quintessence of dust.

Man is the *it* in that sentence.

Woman is *it*.

Man writes down a secret. This way he can keep his secret and still impart it to another. Woman is that other.

Post Time

One clock
of agony one cocked
one's gun.

One ran while
the other clocked
his run.

One man one
woman thy will
be done,

and she be true
though not to you,
old son.

The Hotel Fiesta Sestina

As fingerprints to a detective is a painter's brushstroke
to critics who reveal themselves by their choice of hotel
in foreign cities where the weather is inner
and an impassive tuxedo-clad angel may dance the tango
with a nude in bright hues, and later they get to eat breakfast
in bed and talk about modern art and its wonders.

We needed great paintings in a world without wonders.
But then concepts replaced paintings. It was a masterstroke
some guy in marketing wrote on a napkin at breakfast
where the coffee was weak at the conventioneers' hotel.
Our parents learned dances like the tango.
And what do we do? Nothing. We go inner.

I took a journey into the interior, where your inner
child met the adult I was when I was a boy. Of all wonders
I have known, this still seems to me supreme, this tango
of male and female, stroke and counterstroke,
her dress on a hanger in the closet of the hotel,
near the ocean, nothing fancy, a little bed and breakfast.

The meal of the day the couple craves is breakfast.
He reads the newspaper while her thoughts turn inner.
She does the math. Do two by night in a grand hotel
equal three by day on a beach? Yes, and no wonder
we display the dildo of our truest selves at the stroke
of midnight when we commence upon our last tango.

Every time we dance is the last time we dance the tango.
In the morning, gazes averted, we eat a guilty breakfast.
We stutter like elderly victims of a stroke.
Part of me is still inside you; yet your inner
self's now closed to me, not close to me, and I wonder
if we will ever again consummate our longing in this hotel

where adulterers pretend to be businessmen and hotel
owners' wives turn out to be spies. I loved the tango
of early morning, a big bathtub, lingering breakfast,
and still do, because of you. The wonder
is not that our bodies resist the menacing stroke
of the hours but that the lovers withdraw, go inner.

In an inner chamber at our first hotel
where the tango was a stroke of genius,
you were wonderful, and then we had breakfast.

Desolation Row

The eccentric genius went crazy living by himself.
Few things held his attention.
Spy novels, baseball games on television, Japanese poetry, himself—
the things that used to gladden him now seemed flat or stale.
He felt like Wordsworth, gloomy on a sunny day.
There was a dinner one night. Coleridge sat at one end
of the table and Wordsworth at the other.
Both were talking about poetry. Coleridge was talking
excitedly about a Wordsworth poem. So was Wordsworth.
It was no fun feeling like Wordsworth.
He'd take Coleridge any day lamenting the theft
of his opiated genius by abstruse German philosophy.
"Deprivation is for me what daffodils were for Wordsworth,"
Philip Larkin quipped. But he knew better. There was
only one thing that held his interest now, and that was pornography.
This was after disillusion with the French Revolution
had set in. He thought maybe here was a subject
he could contemplate: disillusionment. Yes,
that's what he would do, that would be
his new project to ward off ennui.

"But Only . . ."

I accompanied him to prison, taking the cell next to his, but only to make sure he wouldn't escape. That was the cover story, but only a credulous fool would believe it. We had taken a tour of chateau towers and church spires, disguising ourselves as clerics, but only to kill the time between assignments. One night as I slept a convention of architects and surveillance experts assembled a model prison in San Francisco but only because the California state legislature was throwing money at the problem of overcrowded correctional facilities. I slept fitfully, awakened by fears or loud neighbors, and decided to stay awake, but only because I had homework to do and now was as good a time as any to do it. A commotion outside caused me to go to the window but only for a few minutes. I opened the window and stuck my head out but only to see whether a revolution had commenced. I could see the eyes of the people in the street below, but only a few of them looked familiar. The people were looking up, but only because of a strong light flashing from the top of the building. There was misery in their eyes, but only because they had forgotten why they had gathered at four in the morning in this inauspicious part of the city.

Les Enfants terribles

In memoriam Judith Moore

When girlfriend and boyfriend begin to find out
What each other is really like:
A poke in the pants leaves the problem unsolved
Like a mystery with too many conflicting clues
And no detective to follow the leads but an off-Broadway
Off-duty cop, well-intentioned but despised
By his unfulfilled wife, ten years his junior,
Who is tired of being a homemaker, and won't have kids,
Which is what he wants, wouldn't you know it,
Whether because he can't get it or not, who can say
Without fear of misrepresentation? Still, living together
As they have, month after month, the years in and out,
They have come to know each other quite as well
As kids growing up in the same room, listening
To the same stupid songs on the radio, inventing new problems
So that, solving them, they can feel like a couple
Of adults at last; and the year cranberries were poisonous
They kept a jar of cranberry sauce in the ice-box
And the first person to eat some was ridiculed
In the ambulance by smarter brother and older sister
Looking as gleeful as a bow-tie on a chubby cigar-smoker's collar.

No doubt it's a miracle they have survived at all
But survive they have, waking up relieved from bad dreams,
"Hey, I don't have poison ivy after all!"

She has learned how to handle his gun, while he has mastered
The cockpit of her plane, and together they ride
Remote-control, handcuffed together for better and for worse.
On a more pedestrian level, things have been working out, too:
A time-saving division of labor has been devised
Whereby she buys the groceries and he does the dishes
And soon they shall become parents themselves
In order to get back at their own, but first
There is a hell of bills to pay, application forms to fill out,
And alarm clocks to obey, cursing. After a year
Of paid unemployment, it's hard to go back to being
A secretary on Wall Street, where the days off are few
And the boss a cheap lecher, but is there any choice?
And the receptionist hates the typist, and the account
Executives hate each other, and the secretaries hate
Themselves, and the file clerk hates the works.

So off they go, on exhausted day off, confined
To the pleasures of local sightseeing, resigned
To study what they used to mock with a child's cruel honesty:
States of sleep, changes of weather, the differing light
Of a New York street in winter. And always with anger
Difficult to deny, though they try, though to what purpose
They do not know. The search for a common enemy
Took them to the city a long time ago, and now
They're stuck. Trying to piece together the plot,
Having come in the middle of the movie, they feel like hollering
At the loud-mouth midget in the seat behind them
For it's no fun punching someone your own size
And there's nothing as delightful as an interrupted argument
To team up with your opponent and let the peacemaker
Take it on the chin, which is what he was leading with,
Let's face it. So many Saturday night movies
They begin to miss the background music
When there isn't any in their lives. What, they wonder,
Are they to do with all that wasted virility,
Those cheap cinematic effects like an unheeded cry
For help, a twisted piano string around the neck, a mother's tears?

And after the picture is over they go to a bar and talk
About the actress they have just seen, feeling like Paris.
"She was a cunt," the man says. "Yes, but she was
A beautiful cunt," the woman replies. *The Sun Also Rises*
Made him want to be a writer in high school, but she
Went to college with Scott Fitzgerald, and memorized
The meaning of romance. Now, half a century later,
She knows the voice rising from deep within his body
Bursting in his throat like a threat
Or the fear of a pair of praying hands
Menacing because detached
From the body they once belonged to—
An executioner on his day off during the Reign of Terror in France.
An infinity of colliding particles is the aftermath of the pill
In the glass of water he swallows, and smiles, and says goodbye
Moments before leaving for his new job at the White House
And he is carrying a briefcase, as is considered good form,
But instead of the papers and the prophylactics
Customarily contained within, he has learned
How to pack his voice like a bomb
And he knows his death is only a few minutes away.

1976

Obit

His art was happy
—Yeats

No art is precise each
depends on errors accidents but
he looked at it with
the neutrality of an aloof
museum guard and secret visionary
of green hills in the south
where he wanted to go
with face and nose pressed
to a sweet-shop window
but who knew his mind?
Born in Russia lived poor
in Paris sold his first
paintings lived with a dancer
as hot tempered as he
and went to California to
die when the twentieth century
was still an impossible future
not yet an important failure.

Money Variations

1.

Money is cock, said the professor.
We live in a phallic society.

Protesters were walking around
holding posters saying,
"Money rules," and
"Money is the market," and
"Money is nonjudgmental," and
"Money is a kind of poetry."
One heckler shouted,
"Where id was, shall money be,"
but the speaker had the wit to reply,
"Where is was, let ego go free."

"Face it, we're a nation of salesmen,"
said the bartender.
"I can't change my fucking address
without someone trying to sell me
a variable annuity."
"Are you changing your address?"
"Yes, but that's not the point,"
he snarled.
"Can I buy you a drink?"

Meanwhile the bearded nebbish next door
was playing James Taylor singing
"You've Got a Friend"
at top capacity and I went over to see
if I could get him to lower the volume.
"Or else," he said.
"Or else," I said,
"You've got an enemy."

Ha! Show me the money!

     2.

It's money that puts the fannies in the seats.
It's money that pays the bills,
Buys the drinks, pays for the pills,
Separates the good guys from the cheats.

It's money that put the monkey on my back,
It's money that can make my monkey fly.
Money is unsentimental and never needs to lie.
Money is only that which we lack.

How to say this? Money is tits,
You either have them or you don't.
Money doesn't care if you will or if you won't.
For money never calls it quits.

For money's the honey that makes the babe talk
Money's the bunny that sat in my lap
Money's the flower that shut like a trap
Money's no dummy that makes the babe walk.

It's money for me and me for you,
It's what we do after we screw,
If false to you, to none can it be true,
It's you for me and money for you.

For money's the color of my true love's hair,
Money's the smell of her in the dark.
In the foreign night where no dogs bark,
Money's the flashlight that leads to her lair.

Curse

Whatever your position, you will reverse it.
You will learn a new language and curse it.
Whatever your father says you'll oppose
and believe you're acting on principle.
If each lie added an inch to your nose
well, pal,
you won't come out smelling like a rose.

And that reminds me: though everyone picks on
the president who succeeded Lyndon Johnson,
the major difference between Richard Nixon
and a character in *The Importance of Being Earnest*
is that Nixon believes his lies
and Wilde's characters know they are fibbing,
they lie with a glint in their eyes,
they enjoy a good ribbing,
and then the falsehoods come true and
Jack who claimed to be Ernest is Ernest
in earnest and wins Joan Greenwood's hand.
And Richard Nixon remains Richard Nixon.

Death, the Theory

The imp of the perverse was a deceiving elf.
The headaches came more often
with other blows the pills couldn't soften.
I was a fat girl once myself.

When I got out of the shower,
the money was missing from my wallet.
I bent down and picked up a spent bullet
with no memory of the previous hour.

The checks and balances were in the mail,
as was a message from my muse.
We bought on the rumor, sold on the news,
and did our time in jail.

Yes, I was the revolutionist
who learns the old order was better.
The weather kept getting wetter.
You could make out two figures in the mist.

The "Quickmuse" Poems

Poem

No breakfast except a cup
of yesterday's leftover coffee
plus my usual cocktail
of vitamins, minerals, chemicals
and placebos and you're already
peppering me with queries
about Ford's pardon of Nixon,
Saddam Hussein hanging,
James Brown dancing,
and Robert Altman talking
when the dead voices I want
to hear sing are those of Anita O'Day
and Betty Comden who died the same day
or maybe just their obits appeared
on the same day in the *Times*
have you ever noticed how many deaths
of old famous people happen in December
that's because God's working overtime
to meet the quota it's easy to believe
the market's up 63.52 but I'm hearing
Anita O'Day sing "Falling in Love with Love"
which Rodgers wrote with Hart
a better way for the day to start

The Real Thing

I don't agree
that dancing solves anything
except how to differentiate
between poetry and prose
the former being to the dance
(gratuitous)
what the latter is to taking a walk
(purposive)
according to Paul Valéry
who felt that an artificial rose
was equal to or better than
the real thing.

I love that phrase: "The Real Thing."
It makes me think
of Henry James's story of that title
and the Coca-Cola commercial
identifying Coke as "the real thing."
If I could write an essay on that unusual
conjunction of names and facts
in fifteen minutes, it's because
you can do a lot in fifteen minutes
such as wash your hands, change the CD
from Anita O'Day to Dinah Shore singing
"Buttons and Bows," and write twenty-five
lines, which for some writers equals their entire
daily allotment. Or you can dance.

The other day I discovered the beginning
of a poem from 1980 handwritten
on a piece of paper tucked into my copy
of William Gass's *On Being Blue*.
The epigraph was from Rilke:
"Dance the Orange."
There are a couple of lines worth saving:

"Dance the skeleton on the doctor's desk."
"Dance the rabbi on one foot explaining the law."

Nevertheless I insist that
James Brown to the contrary notwithstanding
there's no point to it, nothing to gain from dancing,
and that is the great glory of the dance
though some might argue that dance
does have a purpose as the first step
toward mating and the reproduction of the species,
a complicated subject demanding more
than fifteen minutes, but as Ira Gershwin
wrote, I'm dancing and I can't
be bothered now.

Poem in Three Parts

1.

Some dictators who favor military garb
deserve to be hanged I guess but brag
about it I wouldn't as one who opposes
capital punishment and supposes
it's possible to hold contradictory ideas
in the mind and function, etc., aides
permitting. I am dictating into a phone.
Does that make me a dictator? Nope. No hope
for the mighty, no rest for the wicked.
Sooner or later everyone feels dicked.

2.

"You got me crying again," Lee Wiley
sings. She asked me to reconcile
the opposing statements I made and

I did what I usually do I shrugged
and shyly asked "Do I have to?" It's
like defining "the Soviet experiment"
in fifty words or less it can be done but
I'd rather meditate on a number
the number seven for example
seven days in a week and on
the seventh day he rested
in the seventh heaven.

3.

The dictator wrote
novels but the poet
didn't dictate foreign policy.
Is that, as Peggy Lee sang,
"all there is"?

Variations on a Theme

1.

You're in love and you'll do anything
You'll lie beg threaten to join the army
join the army get shot come home
wounded and embittered you'll do it
For a taste of her jam you'll agree to it
Agreed but wisdom isn't survival
well maybe it includes survival but
it isn't only survival it has to exalt
something else such as love
the love that led you
to abandon all wisdom

2.

You're in love
You head down to the river to cry
all lovers have the right to cry
and sing the blues
down around the river

3.

You're in love and Paris
with lover and lust
it's human to want to hear
her voice in your ear
and you quicken your stride
like an electrician on his day off
who knows how the place is wired
and wouldn't let her do something weird
like stick her finger in a socket
and that's why she loves him
and he has taken her to Paris.

—1 / 4 / 07

Homily

Man has the will
to grieve
a week and no longer.

Ever the stranger
he will kill
with righteous anger.

What does he believe?
In his right to trade
a season of greed

for an hour
of love in an unlit corner.
Such is love's power,

though it last no longer.
And such is his need
than which nothing is stronger.

The Kiss

Love is never satisfied. An unperfumed woman
Who comes from everywhere
To the same shower, her chestnut hair
In the air, waving, becomes aware

Of the eyes of a man who covets her
With the lust of a man for his neighbor's wife,
And banishes the fantasy. It is the clean moment
Before children clutter up the house

After the house came into being
With garden walls on which you can read
The handwriting of the past, and not understand it.
It is winter. The shades are drawn.

The world is waiting. The love
Of a man for his father becomes
The love of a son for his son. And the woman
Asleep in the morning of her bedroom.

1972

A Valediction: Forbidding Mourning

You who are the reader
had an identity crisis, went to college
went on strike
but fell out with the movement
when someone started a fire in the library.
You were reading Rousseau at the time.

Hiking in the woods was your pastime.
You sat on a rock and wrote pages no reader
would see. Leaves were your library.
A congress of birds was your college.
They consoled you, told you to strike
up the band when down, play the *scherzo* movement

of a romantic symphony, and observe the movement
of water in the stream marking time
You smoked unfiltered Lucky Strikes.
You defined a writer as a reader
who skipped classes in college,
spent night in bars and days in the library.

One section of your ideal library
has books with blank pages. No movement
of men and arms can stand up to a college
of ideas: you believed that at the time.
You believed in the inalienable rights of the reader,
who could bring down poetry by going on strike.

Like a patient batter taking a first-pitch strike,
the professors assembled on the steps of Low Library,
and talked. Students perused *The Rousseau Reader*.
Some joined an underground movement
of philosophers committed to a new refutation of time.
The course you most wanted to take in college,

"Romanticism from Rousseau to Hitler," an old college
standby, gave way to a course on great strikes
in union history. Like a referee calling time,
the head librarian asked all to observe library
decorum and said that for the sestina movement
to get off the ground, we needed new readers.

Gather round, ye readers, nostalgic for college,
and the concept of timeless truths beyond movements
of protestors striking poses in the photogenic library.

Part Two

The Will to Live

"They say that Schopenhauer is pessimistic. That is not saying very much. [His] is a grandiose and tragic vision which, unfortunately, coincides perfectly with reality."
—Witold Gombrowicz,
A Guide to Philosophy in Six Hours
and Fifteen Minutes

1. Arthur Schopenhauer was a competitive man
   who felt nothing but scorn for Hegel.
   So he scheduled his philosophy lectures
   on the same day and at the same time
   and therefore Hegel had a packed auditorium
   while only a handful of us—a Polish writer,
   an ex-girlfriend, a few wayward apostles
   and I—heard Schopenhauer's lectures
   on Descartes, doubt, and the will to live.

2. Life's a bitch and then you die. Everything proceeds from this
      proposition.

3. Many philosophers, professional sad sacks,
   make merry with women and whiskey at night.
   Not Schopenhauer. He was logical. Eating
   a delicacy like pressed goose livers with
   a good Sauterne proved only that nothing
   exists except the temporary satisfaction

of a hunger that will return and a thirst
without which no liquid tastes good.
Pleasure is merely the absence of pain,
not a thing in itself, and the same may be said
of peace in relation to war. And yet—

4. Look at all the things we need to endure—
death and pain, struggle and fear—
in order for the species to survive,
and so great is our determination to live
that endure these hardships we do, putting
a good face on things, hurricanes
and suicide bombers, the death of adulthood
and the abandonment of the beautiful
English language. And yet—

5. One of the apostles asked about suicides.
What about them, Schopenhauer replied.
"Don't they invalidate your theory
of the will to live?" "Not at all,"
he smiled for once. "In suicide they prove
the will to live is greater than they are."

6. There were two proofs:
(a) God must exist
if we can conceive of God
(b) God must but cannot exist
if we can conceive of that
than which nothing greater
can be or be conceived.
Therefore,
God has to exist
as a logical possibility
impossible to disprove
or credit.
That's what he said.
I wrote it down.

You may think he was
a world-class pessimist
but then you didn't know him
as I did in Berlin
a hundred years before Hitler.

L'Shana Tova

For David Shapiro

I hear the ram's horn.
Do you? Do you remember
father, son, mountain?

L'shana tova
old friend, mentor, fellow Jew,
you from New Jersey,

I from Manhattan,
and we met not in temple
but Columbia

and do you recall
when I visited Cambridge
I left you a note

with the Clare porter.
The world is charged (I wrote) with
the grandeur of you!

And then you came home
and I took your place over
there: at Clare College

Peter Ackroyd came
and asked me if I would speak
to the group on John

Ashbery whose new
book *The Double Dream of Spring*
had just been published.

How could I say no?
They told me you had spoken
on Frank O'Hara

and Aaron Fogel
had spoken on Kenneth Koch.
It was a good omen

I thought but then what
happened was rain rain rain and
more rain. And no mail

because of a strike
in England. There was always
a strike in England.

No mail, no phone calls
to America where my
father lay dying.

The gardeners burned
the leaves and I crossed the Cam
on Clare College bridge

daily, and daily
I went to Heffers and bought
books by Hölderlin,

Mann, Gide, Henry James.
I imitated Rilke.
The sonnet for you

ran in *Poetry*.
More rain. Cold toilet. Bad smell.
And I couldn't find

an English poet
younger than Larkin to like.
No mail. Pub hours.

Beer better than wine.
Awful food. Always hungry.
Had to learn to cook.

And that's where I went
—to the sea of memory—
in temple today

when I heard the sound
of the *shofar* and prayed for
the living and dead.

The Trip Not Taken

> I regret not having taken up the offer of a Cambridge col-
> league, a pathologist of proven insight and tact, to try LSD
> under his supervision. Having experienced no such drug, I
> remain at a loss to imagine, to conceptualise one of the prin-
> cipal agents of ruin and consolation, of desire and annulment
> at the anarchic heart of our culture. A "trip" not taken.
> —George Steiner, *Errata: An Examined Life*

It was in Cambridge in 1970 or 1971 that I went to a lecture
by George Steiner,
an energetic man, who wore his pants too tight
and spoke with an international accent of indeterminate origin.
It was standing room only.
My friends and I stood in the back.
The subject was language and silence
or maybe language versus silence.
Language won.

Steiner praised the American students in Cambridge—
sharper, more daring than the English.
We beamed idiotically.
One of us raised his hand and said something
meant to prove Steiner's point.
He used the words "conceptualize" and "anarchic"
in the same sentence.

My mind was where?
In the girls' dormitory.
Listen to my story.
Nothing could be finer
than to be in her vagina
after listening to George Steiner
at the anarchic heart
of our culture.
Is the heart anarchic?

Nothing could be finer
than to walk among the amber
street lamps of Cambridge
after the lecture
and visit my friend's sister
who brought blotter acid with her
from America
and what we did
we did without supervision
and we didn't own a television
but we owed ourselves a vision
and we had it in front of a store
with women's sweaters in the window
not on King's Parade but the next street over.

I have to tell you: Steiner was brilliant.
And we had the experience
even if we did miss the meaning:
ruin and consolation, desire and
annulment. We took
the trip.

Paris, 1971

In retrospect it was romantic to be the lonely American recovering from pneumonia, living in a hotel room with a typewriter and a sink in a Left Bank hotel in a gray Paris winter.

At the time I was constantly cold, it rained seven days a week, my feet were wet, I was awkward with girls and wanted sex so badly I couldn't sleep at night, in London.

In retrospect I was neither Alyosha nor Ivan, not Orwell in Spain nor Hemingway on a fishing trip nor Henry Miller in Clichy.

At the time I saw *The Wild Bunch,* Sergio Leone's *Duck, You Sucker, The Go-Between, Sunday, Bloody Sunday,* and *Woodstock.*

In retrospect the gloom of the deserted streets and the sound of footfalls were full of strangeness in medieval Cambridge.

At the time I became self-conscious about my American accent. I began pronouncing the t's in words like city or university, and I said to-mah-to at the greengrocer's.

In retrospect I spent more money than my friends did at restaurants like the Koh-I-Noor, the Gardenia on Rose Crescent, and the Rembrandt. Then I learned to cook.

At the time I went to London for the weekend. There was a new place called the Great American Disaster that specialized in hamburgers. I saw John Gielgud in a matinee.

In retrospect I met a Swedish woman named Eva, blonde and beautiful, and the sex was great but we had nothing to talk about and I grew melancholy in the Scandinavian manner.

At the time I moved into an apartment near the Rue des Ecoles with a dandy who had a magnificent cane and liked walking with me to Montparnasse where a couple of Chaplin films were showing.

In retrospect I read "Le Cimetière marin" by Paul Valéry.

At the time I was a naive American in a trench coat and fedora trying to make ends meet in Berlin in the waning days of the Weimar Republic.

In retrospect Beckett and Lorca.

At the time Stravinsky and Frank Zappa.

In retrospect Otto Dix, André Derain, and the Ballets suédois.

At the time the Pompes Funèbres sign between Saint Sulpice and Saint-Placide.

In retrospect we spent hours in the Rond-Point café playing Dipsy Doodle and other pinball machines made by the U.S. manufacturer Williams.

At the time steak tartare with capers and cornichons at Le Drugstore. I was sick for two days after.

In retrospect we went to Le Dôme, La Rotonde, Le Select, La Coupole, and the best of these was Le Dôme.

At the time Nicole asked me to find out whether she could come to England to have an abortion. She was my friend, not my girlfriend. I wasn't responsible.

In retrospect, the English doctor gave me as dirty a look as I've ever faced.

At the time of the Ali-Frazier fight at the Garden a smell like that of peaches wafted in the air, and spring was only weeks away.

In retrospect the Opéra, the Madeleine, the Sainte Chapelle, the Sacré Coeur, the Saint Germain.

At the time the Jockey Club where Lew played piano and we cheered him on—Gail and I and Tim and maybe even Edda.

In retrospect I visited Paul Auster in a garret near the Louvre, which he got with the help of Jacques Dupin.

At the time I read Simenon in French and (on Auster's recommendation) *The Real Life of Sebastian Knight*. He gave me a copy of his poem "Stéle," and Larry Joseph filched it.

In retrospect I began a poem entitled "Interrupted Messages" and left it on my desk. Jonathan Lear came by when I wasn't in and wrote a note on the poem ending in the hope that he hadn't "sullied a vital piece of paper." I liked "sullied."

At the time the blue airmail letter arrived on a Tuesday morning. The in-flight movie on the way home was *Love Story*. I didn't see it. The off-duty flight attendant sitting next to me was engaged to be married to a minor league shortstop from Broken Arrow, Oklahoma.

In retrospect I took French lessons at the Alliance Française and went with a Spanish girl to a movie with Jean Gabin and Simone Signoret as an old quarrelsome married couple.

At the time I watched the little kids sail their toy boats in the Jardin du Luxembourg.

In retrospect I was always alone.

At the time I sat with you in the Bois de Boulogne and we took turns guessing what was in each passerby's mind.

French Movie

I was in a French movie
and had only nine hours to live
and I knew it
not because I planned to take my life
or swallowed a lethal but slow-working
potion meant for a juror
in a mob-related murder trial,
nor did I expect to be assassinated
like a chemical engineer mistaken
for someone important in Milan
or a Jew journalist kidnapped in Pakistan;
no, none of that; no grounds for
suspicion, no murderous plots
centering on me with cryptic phone
messages and clues like a scarf or
lipstick left in the front seat of a car;
and yet I knew I would die
by the end of that day
and I knew it with a dreadful certainty,
and when I walked in the street
and looked in the eyes of the woman
walking toward me I knew that
she knew it, too,
and though I had never seen her before,
I knew she would spend the rest of that day
with me, those nine hours walking,
searching, going into a bookstore in Rome,

smoking a Gitane, and walking,
walking in London, taking the train
to Oxford from Paddington or Cambridge
from Liverpool Street and walking
along the river and across the bridges,
walking, talking, until my nine hours
were up and the black-and-white movie
ended with the single word FIN
in big white letters on a bare black screen.

Existentialism

In postwar New York, *existentialism* was sexy, debonair, chic, and anti-academic. It was either a philosophy or something resembling one, a bundle of linked ideas and assumptions, largely imported from Europe, that attracted the herd of independent minds feeding the cultural discourse on this side of the Atlantic. Advocates quoted Jean-Paul Sartre ("existence precedes essence") and called it an "action philosophy," a survivor's answer to nihilistic despair. Whatever it was, it went well with berets and saxophones, Abstract Expressionists in cold water lofts, and heroes of novels searching for authenticity in a universe of chance, an African desert, the pages of the *Partisan Review,* or a movie theater outside New Orleans.

For a certain extraordinary period of time, everyone wanted to be existential. Not everyone knew what this meant, exactly, but everyone wanted the distinction. Misused and overused, the very word *existential* began to function as a sort of highbrow condiment of choice, the squirt of *moutarde de Dijon* that spiced up the hot dog of a trite observation. It was irresistible. To Norman Mailer, *existential* signified the cool of John F. Kennedy at the Democratic National Convention in Los Angeles in 1960—or maybe it meant a mutual climax achieved by anal intercourse. If you wore sunglasses in the subway and listened to Miles Davis, you were probably existential.

Was there a difference between *existential* and *cool*? Yes. Though it was possible to be both, as the example of Miles Davis attests, there were a lot of cool cats without an existential bone in their bodies. Think of Johnny Carson, or James Bond, or Mickey Mantle. At the same time some bona fide existentialists would bore you stiff if you had to spend an hour in their company at La Coupole or Deux Magots. I feel certain, for example, that an hour of silence with Heidegger, whose existential credentials are impeccable, would be harder to endure than an hour of silence with Wittgenstein or Bertrand Russell.

According to Albert Camus, Algerian-born hero of the French Resistance, practicing existentialism was like fishing in a bathtub. A well-meaning neighbor, thinking to humor the fisherman in the bathtub, says, "Catch anything?" "No, you fool," the fisherman replies. "Can't you see this is a bathtub?" Delmore Schwartz sticks with the tub image. Existentialism, he wrote, means that no one else can take a bath for you.

Some of the greatest moments in the history of existentialism are

- Nietzsche's announcement in *Die fröhliche Wissenschaft* (*The Gay Science*; 1882) that God is dead.

- *Time* magazine's confirmation that God is dead in its cover story of April 8, 1966.

- The moment Jean-Paul Sartre realized that in hell he would have to room with Albert Camus.

- The moment when, in a BBC-TV production of a Sartre novel, a man who has impregnated a young woman, and now, in a fit of conscience and remorse, lifts a cleaver to lop off his offending organ, has second thoughts. "I cannot do it," he says, putting down the cleaver. "I am condemned to be free."

- The moment when David Hemmings as the no-name photographer in Antonioni's *Blow-Up* (1966) retrieves the nonexistent tennis ball that the mime troupe pretends to have lost.

- The moment when the spy played by Richard Burton in his seedy trench coat decides to die with the librarian played by Claire Bloom rather than abandon her on the wrong side of the Berlin Wall and escape to his freedom in the west.

- The first time Herman Melville's Bartleby, an existentialist *avant la lettre,* says, "I would prefer not to," declining to perform a task assigned him by his boss.

- The evening in John Updike's *Rabbit, Run* (1960) when the hero, a young family man, drives off and decides not to return home. The hero's last name, Angstrom, includes the German word for anxiety or dread, *Angst,* which was second only to *alienation* as the term of choice in the bars below 14th Street during those heady postwar days when existentialism ruled the discursive roost.

Existentialism died with the dawning of the age of Aquarius. Relief pitchers began to sport flamboyant mustaches, feminists insisted that the personal was political, Andy Warhol made silkscreen prints of Liz Taylor and Marilyn Monroe, the phrase *Deep Throat* referred first to a porn flick about a blow-job queen and then to a clandestine news source spilling the beans on Watergate, and Lennon and McCartney's "Yesterday" eclipsed Jerome Kern's "All the Things You Are" as the most recorded love song of the twentieth century. All this plus Vietnam, Watergate, and deconstruction spelled the demise of existentialism.

Such perhaps is the fate of certain avant-garde movements in art or thought. They arrive with the intent to move heaven and earth, and after they've gone, what they leave is their faded glamour, and it's the same old hard earth, and heaven's as remote as ever.

The Change

Has anything changed
well, let's take stock
you'd have to say
Gilligan's Island has had
a bigger effect than
Saul Bellow that Miller's
"tastes great" versus "less
filling" commercials for
Lite Beer have entered
our collective consciousness
as has no presidential speech
since Nixon resigned
and the *Times* reports
a lot of people think
"self-esteem" is spelled "self of steam"
so I guess the answer
to your question is clear
nothing's different it's still
Nietzsche versus nurture

On Humility

Kenneth Koch was right:
Why crave the approval of
critics: if you could

see them as they really
are, you wouldn't give a damn
what in hell they think.

Isaac B. Singer
said a man who wants a prize
doesn't deserve one.

Such humility
may be rare but is the right
path for the poet.

"I wasn't handed
anything on a platter":
Universal dad.

Best to lead your life
as if you must leave the house
and never come back.

To buy cigarettes
no longer a good excuse
yet still weirdly apt.

Your life could be a
novel waiting to happen
when you walk into

your destiny: a
bank during a robbery:
courage or folly

are the choices you
have: whether 'tis nobler to
show grace or survive:

whenever I use
colons as in these stanzas
I think of Archie

Ammons, whose name is
split between stanzas here as
Ben Jonson did it.

To name the absent
friend and thus bring that person
back is one purpose

of poetry, one
reason we write beyond
the sheer joy of it.

Ben Jonson put his
full name into a poem
before Whitman did.

Can you think of an
earlier example? I
can't, but the slant of

sunlight on the house
across the street has all
my attention now.

And down goes the sun.
The tall pines darken again.
Gone the orange light.

Ambivalence

Say we walk at the pace of the lame
in a gaudy city without walls,
a lit match for two, a contest of wills:
would there be journalism in our future?

Would reporters continue to defame
our leaders and would a hollow
laugh sound its echo? My shirt's a shadow
though I know there is no blackness in nature.

Of fears the fear of failure is the least
to which we cling beyond the schism
to which we cannot compare the pornography of Fascism
or live in the castle without angst like a beast.

God Will Provide

There's mein Vater
Mit nacht und wind

Forgive me father
I have sinned

There's the book
(Bis du verrückt)

There's my fear
Is rescue near

There's the choir
Where's my father

There's the house
Where's the fire

There's the fire
Where's the lamb

There's the knife
Where's the ram

There's my supper
Where's meine Mutter

There's the mountain
Where's die Stimme

Um Gottes willen
Where's the villain

There's the angel
Where's the hero

There's the ruin
Where's the temple

Days of Penitence and Awe

In temple I prayed
and chanted Holy! Holy!
Holy! And was scared.

Father forgive me.
For what? For things done, not done.
The time I wasted.

For "scared," read "sacred,"
its anagram. I am, said
the Lord. The terror!

The terror! Isaac
knew it. But do we? Faithless
friends exit the scene

after wasting years
playing Falstaff drinking and
praising his own past.

He believed in what?
In Prince Hal, who loved him but
had to reject him.

What do we believe?
Money money money said
Roethke and Lawrence.

We believe that life in
an office is hard work and
a cocktail at five.

We believe in pills.
Chemistry and medicine
can make us young. Vanity

fair as life is not.
We believe there are two outs,
bottom of the ninth.

Bottom of the night.
Vulgarity supreme, a
loud new century

of madmen in robes.
People have asked me what is
my favorite word.

I say "you." Sometimes
I think the most potent word
in English is "Jew."

O could I absent
myself from my daily rounds!
I would return as

the count of Monte
Cristo or Joseph revealed.
So I fondly dream.

Just so my mind roams
while the rest of me sits here
in temple and prays.

God: A Sestina

God
in the splendor of his absence
cajoled argued
refused to believe
the news denied
it was a hoax.

Call off the hoax,
he said. You can't copyright God.
The judge denied
the appeal. The absence
of evidence argued
for ambiguity. Yet you believe.

In what do you believe?
In the value of a hoax.
It's as philosophers have long argued
concerning the existence of God.
The consensus is his absence
will go on. Motion to dismiss denied.

But some things can't be denied.
The inventive power of belief,
in the void left by the absence
of divinity, can hatch a hoax
overnight while the shadow of God
slips in and out of learned argument.

After hours of argument
the priests defy rather than deify,
and God
escapes the belief-
system, reduced to a hoax,
a feat of rhetoric disguising the absence

that surrounds us as if the absence
were real as air and not fake as an argument
no one wins because it was a hoax
and because the debaters claimed deniability
for themselves and banishment for believers
in the old wrathful all-knowing God

One theory: God enjoyed a clever hoax
but denied planning his absence in advance
and argued for a suspension of disbelief.

Prophecy

No waste of shame, no wilting of the flower,
the stick shall not break,
the bat shall not splinter,
no friend will wake, no end of winter;

nor remembrance of splendor
to counter the paper bull's power
will cover the lake with ice
when gamblers spill the dice:

the mirror shall not tilt,
the quick shall not hinder,
nor witness to detect the trick
that cured the sick in their chamber

where clerks of art shall light the wick
of candles that shall never burn
as disputatious churchmen learn
the lesson of the mortar, blood of the brick.

Yeshiva Boys

1. The Ten Plagues

Came the plagues and we named them in order:
blood, frogs, lice, wild animals, pestilence, boils, hail,
locusts, darkness, and the slaying of the first born.

The scholars agree that hail was,
except for the slaying of the first born,
the most devastating of the ten.

Yet Pharaoh did not relent,
and the Egyptians knew not Joseph,
and God did not repent of his work.

The boys made the transition from Genesis
to Exodus when the infant Moses burned his tongue
on hot coals and spoke thereafter with a stammer.

All of a sudden there was a funny smell
that probably came from outside the room.
Since you all say it came from outside,

I shall assume that it came from within,
said Rabbi Kafka. The logic was unassailable
but what caused the smell that made the boys laugh?

If the *chutzpadik* does not stand up now,
you will all suffer, I can promise you that.
He folded his hands. We have ways of making you talk.

2. Rabbi Kafka

Rabbi Kafka asked the class whether the absence
of God dealt a fatal blow to religion.
If God is dead, is everything permitted?

Kalman Kurtz, the butcher's son, spoke first.
"Isn't it the other way around?" he asked.
"God is dead, because everything is permitted."

The boys in the back row traded baseball cards and
cigarettes and first-day-covers. Joshua Freundlich, who had old parents
and was the first among us to wear glasses, raised his hand:

"It's Nietzsche's fault." Not that God was dead but
morality was a hoax hatched by hook-nosed Jews,
the Jew as ugly Socrates, the weakling with the brain

who killed tragedy as surely as Plato expelled the poets
from the Republic. "The Nazis went where Nietzsche pointed:
a land beyond good and evil, during the twilight

of the idols." Reuben Ascher concurred. "For what is Fascism
but the glory of the all-conquering will, the rapist's conquest
of the anus?" Naftali Simon said: "They burned

the books. Action was language minus memory
and meaning, which is one reason Hitler resolved
never to write a thing down if he could say it."

Ephraim Menashe argued that the idea at the core
of Fascism is nihilism. "Then you're at sea and at the mercy
of any lifeboat that comes along." But Ezra Nehemiah interrupted.

"It's Heidegger's fault," he said, and would have said more if not for
the laughter that broke out from the back row of Rabbi Kafka's class.
One boy stood up. He said his name was Philip Roth and his fly

was open. "It's Rabbi Kafka's fault," he said. Then he walked
to the blackboard and erased it. Pandemonium. The very word
brought to mind a congress of devils at a war conference in hell.

In the commotion Kafka seized his chance to slip away.
Let the starving artist make a virtue of his need: Let him fast.
That is his art. And thus Kafka's Hunger Artist was born.

Crowds at his cage in the carnival
admired him. "But you shouldn't admire me,"
he said, dying. "And why shouldn't we?"

"Because I could never find the food that I liked!
If I had, I'd have stuffed my face like you and everyone else."
What a fellow he was! The attendant tossed a steak

to the panther in the next cage, in whose jaws
and flashing teeth you could see the essence of freedom,
while the hero, expiring, was only submitting to necessity.

Rabbi Kafka escaped to Mexico. Details are sketchy.
And Philip Roth died young, a sailor
in the battle of Okinawa in 1945.

3. This Be the Bread

The exodus from Egypt
took place again last night
This is the bread

of affliction this the wine
like the water of the Nile parting
to let the people go

and they went to diverse places
each with a mark on his forehead
like the mark of Cain, progenitor

of the race, an invisible sign by which gentiles
the world over would recognize
the wandering *juif* without his yellow star

always the same story we prayed we fasted
we put on our prayer shawls and phylacteries
and got beaten up by the goyim

and then we went to Lodz
which became the second largest
Jewish ghetto in Europe

and is now the largest Jewish
graveyard in Europe but
when we arrived the gates

were shut so we went
to the Holocaust memorial
the shape of an oven

deserted except for a couple
of kids smoking and necking
and we went inside and walked

down corridors of statistics
and photographs on the walls
born 1938 died 1943

terminating in a yard
of railway tracks a platform
and cattle car to Auschwitz

4. After Auschwitz

In the yeshiva playground they were marching
chanting marching around in circles bearing pickets
bearing scrolls saying "No poems after Auschwitz! No poems

about Auschwitz!" while in the back row
the poet sat dreamily and stared out the window, hungry.
Could there be lunch after Auschwitz?

His mother did everything she could have done
but there wasn't money enough for the necessary bribes
and her parents were deported to Riga and shot.

A woman he met at a writer's conference
told him she was working on *The Holocaust and Memory*
at Yale. The question she had was this:

Are American Jews making a fetish out of the Holocaust?
Has the Holocaust become the whole of Jewish experience?
"You go to shul on Yom Kippur or Passover

and everything is the Holocaust." I shut my eyes and hear
the old prayers made new: *"Shame is real,"* said Ida Noise.
Hear, O Israel. The Lord is One. I, an American, naturally preferred

a temple carved out of water and stone: the rage of a waterfall,
the melody of a brook. But back-to-nature as a strategy failed
when the phones started ringing in the woods,

and only a child would think of collecting dead leaves
and trying to paste them back on the trees. So I returned
to the city, married, settled down, had a child of my own,

pretended that I was just like anybody else.
Yet I feel as if my real life is somewhere else, I left it
back in 1938, it happened already and yet it's still going on,

only it's going on without me, I'm merely an observer
in a trench coat, and if there were some way I could enter
the newsreel of rain that is Europe, some way I could return

to the year where I left my life behind,
it would be dear enough to me, danger and all. *To him,
an emissary of a foreign war, London was unreal. He wondered*

*which of his fellow passengers would make the attempt.
He knew now that they would try to kill him,
tomorrow if not today. How could he have been such a fool?*

*Herr Endlich said: "We have our ways of making a man talk."
In the last forty-eight hours he had learned two things:
That you couldn't escape the danger, it was all around you,*

and that the person who betrays you is the one you trusted most.
The strategists in Washington couldn't figure it out. Why in hell
were the Germans wasting fuel on trains to camps in Poland?

5. Sabbath Feast

How beautiful to me are the red fire escapes of my youth.

How goodly to me are the tents of morning housing the tenants of dry seasons in books read and read again until mastered in old age by tigers who crouch at the edge of the jungle ready to pounce.

How happy the wife who prepares the Sabbath feast.

How happy the son who knows by heart the benediction following the meal.

How happy the daughters who recite the verses of the Bible for their father's pleasure. This week Jacob wrestles the angel of God to a standstill.

How purple the stain of the wine on the white tablecloth, how sweet the ruby wine, how cool the taste on the lips and tongue, how full of zest the grape as it bursts into life in the mouth.

How savory with salt the yellow bread, broken into pieces and blessed, and eaten standing up.

How sweet to the man are the days of his youth. How surprised he would be, could he hear his own voice clamoring for attention at the dinner table with his parents and sisters and perhaps an uncle and aunt on a Friday night in 1961.

6. Intelligence

It's at this point in the picture that the man laughs
and says to the woman, go ahead, pull the trigger.
You'll be doing me a favor. But she can't. She loves him

too much. There's a surprise ending,
but it's the same surprise they used the last time.
The butler did it: in this case, a book editor named Judith Butler.

Days of 1971. The railway stations looked like cathedrals
and though people said Europe had changed in outward ways,
Spain was still fascist and Vienna still full of Nazis.

How long ago it seems. I missed New York terribly,
though I had learned to love the fog of London in which
you could disappear into your anxiety and no one

would notice. I had a very good cover as a fellowship student
in comparative literature at Cambridge, and few guessed
the true nature of my employment in those years when

the Cold War was still frigid. I was in the Culture
Department. The French Resistance was something
we had cooked up to make the French feel less shame.

We came up with theories. It was religion that made it easy to sin.
Or: The path to her panties was lubricated with gin.
Or: The Cold War was something we could win.

In a shabby office near the Luxembourg Gardens
sat Rodgers, a blond man in his thirties
who had gone to Princeton and recruited me.

I reported on the growing hostility
of young French intellectuals
to Israel. Jews who opposed Israel were OK.

They're bitching about us left and right.
The French right can't stand Jimmy Carter
Some crank out there is writing

that the Holocaust never happened
and the left is getting ready to defend him
on freedom-of-speech grounds.

A lot of sentences began, "You Americans."
You Americans are like California babes
with a clitoris where the mind should be.

You Americans with your loud stupid voices
are too soft or too innocent or too ignorant
or all three. You have a lesson coming to you.

But we knew better, savoring our melon with port.
"All painting," said Renoir, "is in the pink ribbon
on the dress of the Infanta." The nights were short,

and there was always time for one more drink. Everyone
had a part to play, and when the fistfight broke out at the pub,
I was the American, derided by all, trying to make peace between

the feuding Europeans. So years went by. In intelligence work
you learn to be tolerant of most people who lead
delusional lives, being unaware of the secret

you carry like a code or a dead language, and
that will die with you because you never revealed it
in all the pages you typed in hotel rooms in Europe.

7. The Categorical Imperative

But then we returned to the present
where Reb Gamliel, known for his strictness,
would examine each of us in turn solo in

his chambers with Reb Nachbar on hand to smile
encouragingly at each bewildered boy asked to parse
a sentence from the Talmud. My sentence concerned

Hillel's questions about biblical proscriptions and whether
the decree against murder applied in the case of an oppressor,
an executioner or assassin. "And what do *you* think?"

Reb Gamliel asked me gravely. And I, who had opinions
about everything, said, "look at the uprising
in the Warsaw Ghetto. They had to fight, for

isn't it better to die in battle than be herded off in boxcars,
to be starved and beaten and finally gassed and burned?"
By this they knew I wasn't long for the yeshiva.

The two rabbis looked at each other with faint smiles.
And when they ushered me out of the room with
congratulatory handshakes and the promise of a high mark,

I was not deceived. I knew my future lay elsewhere
and I let it come rushing at me as an unsuspecting motorist
lets the landscape advance, who sits behind the wheel

of a vehicle that would explode upon impact
with another if both were traveling at sixty-five miles per hour,
going in opposite directions, having left home at the same time.

8. Action Painting

Rabbi Greenberg advocated abstract painting.
Rabbi Rosenberg called it action painting
Rabbi Kline had us study Chinese calligraphy.

My next assignment was to explain
the enduring appeal of Communism
to Italian workers, French students, and English departments.

I don't get it, Rodgers said.
There's nothing more boring than Communism.
Communism means long lines for bread and longer ones for shoes.

What do they see in it?
The Red army let the Nazis raze Warsaw. Then they entered.
He stood at the curtain's edge and looked out the window.

Are you sure you weren't followed?
So I went to Munich, to Milan and to Rome.
Munich in '72 was Israel's first and gravest military defeat.

There's a new enemy.
You can call them terrorists, but then
you'd be defining them by their tactics

and leaving unstated the ideology
behind them. Was it nihilism
as in the anarchist days of Joseph Conrad's

The Secret Agent, or was there something
malignant and medieval on the horizon?
Langley was still fixated on the Soviets

the year the Americans were held hostage
in Teheran, and the Russians invaded Afghanistan.
The center of gravity was about to move

from Berlin to Jerusalem
from Marxism to Muslim fanaticism
and what are you going to do about it, paint an abstract canvas?

9. Safe House

The black seeds on the fresh pink watermelon
looked like flies, and biscotti were served.
The Turin gang was up to something. Rumors

circulated that the next wave of terror attacks
would involve the kidnapping of industrialists
and high-profile politicians whose ears

would fall victim to the executioner's shears
if an outlandish ransom weren't paid. I rented a room
from a schoolteacher in Padua where I'd gone

ostensibly for the Giottos, so blue, but in actuality because
the Turin gang's number two man was said to be
hiding out there. Nothing much happened. I had an affair

with the schoolteacher, who worked miracles in the kitchen
and was pretty, with brown bangs and dark brown eyes.
She had a four-year-old we would take to the park.

Once or twice I had the impulse to fabricate
an incident or a conspiracy in my monthly report.
The codes were elaborate and it took hours to send

even a simple message. For example, "the Colosseum
will be a handsome building when it's finished"
meant "no change," while "the meaner the convent cell,

the richer the convent chapel" translated as
"suspect Padua a bum steer."
Then one day they found Rodgers in his Paris office

with his throat slashed. I left Italy
for the safe house in Zurich where a face as grim
as mine poured brandy and ordered me back to Britain.

The worst was when I met his widow, but
it was a hell of a lot better than Tu Do Street in Saigon.
And what's more, I got to read the surrealists and write bad poems.

My mistress's eyes were almonds, her breasts
were apricots, and her shapely ass was a picnic basket
loaded with cheese, a baguette, and a bottle of wine.

10. The Red Death

Arthur Schopenhauer, Rabbi Biegeleisen's favorite student,
stood up and said he was awestruck at the power
of the will to live, the urge to mate,

despite the misery and pain of human existence.
And so Schopenhauer became known as a pessimist, though
it seems like good old-fashioned horse sense to me, said Beth Hayes.

And God said *be frutiful and multiply.*
This was God's first command.
And just to sweeten the deal, you get to fornicate

like beasts but with the capacity to think about it
afterwards, in secret in the dark, with remembered pleasure
or shame or guilt or love of the one you have linked with.

Nihilism is dead as Utopia is nowhere
and high school sucks but it's better than the old country.
You can always treat yourself to an existential crisis.

God made man in his own image, and man
instantly returned the favor. Did Voltaire say that?
And darkness moved upon the face of the waters.

Next door they were practicing. They had
simulated the camp down to the last detail,
the barbed wire that electrocuted you if you touched it.

And I stood hatless in the wind of the Lord
and saw from the mountaintop what the new year held.
And one by one dropped the revelers

in the blood-bedewed halls of their revels
and died each in the despairing posture of his fall.
And Darkness and Decay and the Red Death held illimitable
dominion over all.

11. The Wrong Man

My Cambridge don waxed eloquent.
"As the *marabout* on his African dunghill
promises a *Mahdi* to the dejected Bedouin,

so the Jews of the diaspora embraced
mystical heresies, counted the days
to the Millennium, or discovered the Messiah."

I met her every Wednesday for a year.
How can you blame me for falling
in love with her? I still have a lock of her hair.

It was the year the Berlin Wall came down
and the Ayatollah issued his fatwa
targeting a blasphemous Muslim novelist.

The information I had could get me killed.
The Sunnis were bad enough
But this new bunch was something else again.

They felt they could terrorize Europe in ten
years, tops. Anti-Semitism is a beautiful thing,
said M. It can even exist without Jews.

They laughed. Fifty years after the Holocaust,
and charming rogue profs at Brown or Penn
quipped, "There's no business like Shoah business."

It took me a day and a half to decode the message,
a page torn out of a spy novel from an earlier era.
"The last thing he expected was to be arrested

at the Spanish Steps and held in jail for a year
on drug charges." The waiting was terrible.
My contact turned up finally and led me

to a blue Fiat beside a ditch near a cement factory
with a body full of bullets in the boot.
"You bloody fool! You've killed the wrong man."

12. Preparing to Meet the Maker

The maker of paradoxes, asked to expose
his worst fears and ours, omits the roses
and stars and Spanish wars and guitars

on Venetian balconies. Instead of an epiphany,
he offers the heightened sense of perplexity
that hunger artists have wished on us in pity,

and we love them for it, before dying
in their arms, like a chastened Cordelia, crying—
but with her innocence intact. Asked to expose

the secret agenda of our nightmares, the boy
in the back row says everything's up for grabs,
negotiable, "on the table," but first we must decide

the shape of the table, and time is running out.
He has a sense of humor, and a headache.
He never got over the problem of evil, the problem of

the philosopher's brown shirt, and the irrational
nostalgia a man of forty feels for his childhood,
which was full of torment at the time.

To those who phone him, asking for a quote,
the maker of paradoxes is unfailingly polite.
He knows there is nothing else he can do.

Epilogue

"When I was born the third child to my parents, they were not over-joyed, since they already had a daughter and a son. But my mother told me I was so pretty that they didn't mind too much.

"We lived in Vienna in the 16th district. It was not a very Jewish dis-trict. Jews lived mostly in the 2nd and 20th districts. And in my class in school were only three Jewish girls out of thirty students. Of course from an early time we were made to feel different. Yet I had many gentile girl-friends and I remember one of them I was pretty close to. Her parents had a little garden with a hut in the outskirts of Vienna and she invited me to sleep over. Yet when Hitler came to power and I met her on the street, she acted funny and held her hand over her bosom until I found out she was wearing a swastika! This was years before Hitler overran Austria—she must have been an underground member in order to have the swastika. This gave me a real shock.

"The police came one day and asked for Adolf. They had orders to take him to the police station. Why, we asked. We need him as a witness, they said. He was present at an accident, they said. We told them: as soon as he comes home we shall send him to the police station. But of course when Adolf came home he told us there had been no accident. He was on a list. The Nazis wanted to send him to a camp. You see, Adolf was the president of some idealistic university organization, a good socialist. And from that day on, he went underground until he got a visa to go to America.

"It was a nightmare to live in Vienna at that time. Every time the doorbell rang, we were afraid—*they're coming for us!*

"A friend of mine got me a permit to go to England as a mother's helper. This way I got out of Nazi Germany. These people, Wright was their name, lived in Southsea. He was a shipbuilder and she was a dentist. They treated me very well, and he gave me English lessons every day. But I was lonely there, so after a few months I went to London, where I had some friends from Vienna. My friend Trude and I found work in the home of an English theatre producer by the name of French. Trude was supposed to be the cook and I was the parlor maid. Once Rex Harrison came to dinner. He was very friendly, a real gentleman.

"I was in England when the war started and we all received the gas masks and instructions for the air raid shelters. The American consulate closed and we had to move to a refugee home. When I saw how bad the situation was and my parents were still in Vienna, I tried to get them out to England. For America they had to wait too long, their quota was very small, since my parents were born in Poland. And we did not know when Hitler came how important it was to be registered in the American consulate. In March 1938 Adolf went to register himself and in April Bert went. I only went in June to register, but at least while I was there I also got the papers to register my parents. Later I found out that each month meant one more year to wait for the visa. But it took even longer if you were born in Poland. So I asked the French people and they filled out a lot of papers which would have enabled my parents to come to England. Everything took so long, when I finally got everything together England was at war and my parents couldn't come. I had no way of getting in touch with them.

"But the American consulate finally opened its door again and I received my visa to go to America. How happy I was. Naturally I was worried to travel on an English ship, so my cousin from America sent me additional money and I changed my ticket to an American ship, the *President Harding*. I think it was the last Atlantic crossing it ever made. It took us ten days of the most terrible shaking. Everyone on board was sick and wanted to die. We were so sick that we weren't even afraid of hidden mines, and as in a dream we did all the safe drillings, etc. The last day was Thanksgiving. We had, and for me it was the first time, a delicious Thanksgiving dinner with turkey and all the trimmings, they played 'Oh, say, can you see,' and when I finally saw the Statue of Liberty, I was really grateful to God, that he let me live and see America."

Acknowledgments and Notes

Heartfelt thanks go to Jim Cummins, Amy Gerstler, Judith Hall, Glen Hartley, Stacey Harwood, and David Shapiro. Editors of literary magazines who commissioned a poem, or helped me improve one, include Richard Burgin, Laurence Goldstein, Eve Grubin, Willard Spiegelman, Christian Wiman, and Joanna Yas. I am especially grateful to Alexis Gargagliano, my editor at Scribner, for her support and astute advice.

Grateful acknowledgment is made of the magazines in which the poems assembled here, or earlier versions of them, appeared: *AGNI, Alaska Quarterly Review,* the *American Scholar, Antioch Review, American Poetry Review, The Atlantic, Barrow Street, Boulevard, Columbia, Coconut,* the *Hat, LIT, Margie, McSweeney's, Michigan Quarterly Review, New American Writing, New England Review,* Nextbook *No Tell Motel, Open City,* the *Paris Review, Poetry, Quickmuse, Smartish Pace, Southwest Review, Tikkun, Times Literary Supplement, Verse.*

"The Quickmuse Poems" were written in one sixty-minute stretch on January 4, 2007. Ken Gordon of the Quickmuse website gave me and fellow poet Kevin Young four prompts and allowed us fifteen minutes to write a poem on each. The prompts were quotes from or about Robert Altman, James Brown, Saddam Hussein, and Gerald Ford, all of whom died toward the end of 2006. Brown was quoted to the effect that dancing is "the one thing that can solve most of our problems." According to Altman, wisdom and love are opposed: "You're wise if you don't stick your finger in the light plug. Love—you'll stick your finger in anything." The other two prompts concerned the hanging of Saddam Hussein, who had written novels, and Gerald Ford's pardoning of Richard Nixon. The poems Kevin and I wrote in fifteen-minute sessions that day are posted on the website www.quickstroke.com, with our real-time key strokes preserved; the poems were also published in *New American Writing*.

The voice in the epilogue is that of my mother, Anne Lehman, born in Vienna in 1915.

About the Author

David Lehman is the general editor of the *Best American Poetry* series, the editor of *The Oxford Book of American Poetry,* and the author of seven books of poetry, including *When a Woman Loves a Man.* The most recent of his prose books is *A Fine Romance: Jewish Songwriters, American Songs* (2009). He lives in New York City.

A Note on the Type

The typeface used for the poetry herein is Sabon, as designed in 1964 by the German typographer Jan Tschichold (1902–1974). Tschichold was challenged to design Sabon for use with the three major machines used to cast hot metal type: full-type line-casting composition machines for the Linotype Corporation, single-character-casting composition machines for the Monotype Corporation, and single-character or foundry type used in hand setting composition for the Stempel Corporation. Sabon, a practical, multipurpose typeface with nonoverlapping characters, is noted for its legibility and grace. Tschichold based Sabon on the type designs of the French Typeface designers Claude Garamond (1480–1561) for the roman and Robert Granjon (1513–1589) for the italic. Sabon is named after Jacques Sabon, the original typefounder of Garamond's version of this typeface.

Berling, the display typeface used herein, was designed from 1951 to 1958 by the Swiss type designer Karl Erik Forsberg for the Berling foundry.

Printed in the United States
By Bookmasters